SURPRISING
SCIENCE

Roller Coasters

Dana Meachen Rau

Marshall Cavendish
Benchmark
New York

For Charlie, my no-fear coaster fan
—D.M.R.

With thanks to James Battat, Pappalardo Fellow in Physics, Massachusetts Institute of Technology, Cambridge, Massachusetts, for the careful review of this manuscript

Other Marshall Cavendish Offices:
Marshall Cavendish International (Asia) Private Limited, 1 New Industrial Road, Singapore 536196 • Marshall Cavendish International (Thailand) Co Ltd. 253 Asoke, 12th Flr, Sukhumvit 21 Road, Klongtoey Nua, Wattana, Bangkok 10110, Thailand • Marshall Cavendish (Malaysia) Sdn Bhd, Times Subang, Lot 46, Subang Hi-Tech Industrial Park, Batu Tiga, 40000 Shah Alam, Selangor Darul Ehsan, Malaysia

Marshall Cavendish is a trademark of Times Publishing Limited.

All websites were available and accurate when this book was sent to press.

Editor: Christina Gardeski
Publisher: Michelle Bisson
Art Director: Anahid Hamparian
Series Designer: Virginia Pope

Printed in Malaysia (T)
1 3 5 6 4 2

Library of Congress Cataloging-in-Publication Data
Rau, Dana Meachen, 1971–
Roller coasters / by Dana Meachen Rau.
p. cm. — (Bookworms chapter books: surprising science)
Includes bibliographical references and index.
Summary: "Discusses the basic scientific principles and historical context of roller coasters"—Provided by publisher.
ISBN 978-0-7614-4872-3
1. Roller coasters—Juvenile literature. I. Title.
GV1860.R64R38 2011
791.06'8--dc22
2009053722

Photo research by Connie Gardner

Cover photo by Lester Lefkowitz/Getty Images

The photographs in this book are used by permission and through the courtesy of: *Getty Images*: pp. 4(L), 8(L), 14(L), 18(L) Lester Lefkowitz; p. 6 Hill Street Studios; p. 7 Lisa Kimmeli; p. 8(R) Roger Violett. *Corbis*: pp. 1, 11 Kevin Flemming. *The Image Works*: p. 3 Museum of London; p. 4(R) Harry DiOrio; p. 9 Roger Violett; p. 10 Mary Evans Picture Library; p. 16 Fujifotos; p. 21(R) Tom Bushey. *SuperStock*: p. 5 Kwame Zikomo. *Alamy*: p. 15 Cernan Elias; p. 21(L) Gabe Palmer. *PhotoEdit*: p. 14(R) Mark Richards; p. 17 Bill Bachmann. *AP Photo*: p. 12 The Daily Citizen, Samuel Peebles; p. 13 Mike Derer; p. 18(R) Tom Dejak; p. 19 Paul M. Walsh; p. 20 Pooley.

Roller Coasters

Rise up to the sky, then race down to the ground. Roller coasters take your breath away!

A Wild Ride

It is hard to wait. But you have to wait at an **amusement park**. The rides are so fun. Everyone wants a turn. You stand in line for an hour. You move closer to the entrance. Finally, you are there!

Climb into the roller coaster car and pull down the **lap bar**. Your car leaves the station and creeps to the bottom of the first hill. You might

Are you sure you don't want to hold on?

6

Twists and turns make for
an exciting ride!

Rides are fun for every age.

hear clanking as the car is pulled up toward the clouds. You feel on top of the world!

Then you suddenly shoot toward the ground. You feel like you are falling as your car races down the hill. You scream with excitement. The car speeds right up the next hill. You zoom up and down through the coaster. You race under and over the tracks. The whole ride might only last a minute or two. But it sure is worth the wait!

CHAPTER 2

Some early coasters, like this one in France, were called scenic railways.

Roller Coaster History

People have always enjoyed the thrill of going downhill. The Russians were the first to build rides like roller coasters in the mid–1600s. A thick layer of ice covered tall wooden ramps. People rode

On early coasters, you climbed a tower and rode the car down a hill.

down the slide on a sled made of ice or wood. The French built the next early coasters in the 1800s. They rode on cars with wheels locked onto a track that sloped down from a tower.

9

In 1884 in New York, the Coney Island amusement park opened the Thompson's Switchback Railway. This ride had two tracks **parallel** to each other with towers at each end. Riders

View of Pier from Steeple Chase, Coney Island, N. Y.

Coney Island in New York became the model for many amusement parks in America.

climbed the stairs to the top of one tower. They rode a car down the hill to the bottom of the other tower. Then they climbed up the second tower. They took another car back to the first. Workmen had to push the cars back to the start after every ride.

Early roller coasters were not very exciting. They moved slowly past **dioramas** along the sides of the tracks. People cared more about the pictures than the ride.

The Mean Streak is a wooden coaster at Cedar Point Amusement Park in Ohio. Wooden coasters are known for their bumpy rides.

More amusement parks opened, and **designers** made roller coasters better and safer. They added more hills, turns, and loops. Thousands of coasters were built in the 1920s. Some people call this time the Golden Age of roller coasters.

On a loop coaster, you get to view the world upside down!

In 1955, Disneyland opened in California. Its roller coaster, the Matterhorn, was built in 1959 and had tracks made from steel tubes. In the past, coasters were made mostly of wood. Wooden coasters gave a rough, bouncy ride. Steel tracks could bend and curve. A ride on a steel coaster was quiet and smooth.

With steel, designers made rides faster and more exciting. Starting in the 1970s, parks tried lots of designs. Corkscrews had a **spiral** shape.

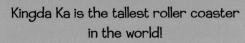

Kingda Ka is the tallest roller coaster in the world!

Riders sped through loops forward and backward. Cars might hang below the track instead of riding on top. Some coasters had no floor. Riders' feet dangled into the open air.

Steel coasters also grew higher. Today, the tallest and fastest coaster is Kingda Ka in New Jersey. It is more than 450 feet high. That's taller than the Statue of Liberty. Many people still enjoy wooden coasters, too. They don't mind being banged around!

CHAPTER 3

Ahhhh! Watch out for gravity!

How Roller Coasters Work

We can look to a science called **physics** to understand how roller coasters work. Physics is the study of how objects move.

During a ride, a roller coaster moves downhill because of **gravity**. Gravity is a force that attracts objects together. The Earth has gravity. If you let go of a ball, it will fall down because the ball is attracted to the Earth by gravity. When gravity pulls on a roller coaster car, the car goes down the hill.

But how does a roller coaster car get up a hill? A chain on the first hill runs in a loop from the bottom to the top and back again. A **motor** makes this chain move. The bottom of the car catches onto the chain. The chain lifts the car along the track to the top of

Do not stand up

Do not stand up

15

A chain pulls a roller coaster car to the top of the first hill.

the hill. At the top, the car lets go of the chain. The car zooms down the other side. Some newer coasters don't have a chain to pull the car up the first hill. Instead, a machine at the station **launches** the car like

Amusement parks can be in the middle of cities, like this one in Tokyo, Japan.

a slingshot. The car has enough speed to get up the hill.

How does the car keep moving up the next hill? Why doesn't gravity keep the car from going up? When the car goes down the first hill, it gains enough **energy** to make it up the second hill. That's because the second hill is shorter than the first. In fact, the car has enough energy to make it over all the hills of the coaster as long as they are shorter than the first, tallest hill. During the ride, you move faster, then slower, then faster, then slower. You gain speed going down a hill. You slow down going up.

Some roller coasters have loops. Imagine you are outdoors holding

Centripetal force keeps a car on a track when it goes around a loop.

a pail filled with water. If you flipped the pail upside down, the water would spill out. That's because gravity pulls the water down to the ground. What if you swung the pail of water in a circle very fast? The water wouldn't spill out! You don't fall out of the car when you go through a loop on a roller coaster either.

How can this happen? **Centripetal force** keeps you in your seat. When objects move forward, they try to move in a straight line. A loop is not a straight line. The roller coaster car takes you around the loop. Your body still tries to move in a straight line. Your body pushes toward the bottom of the car. You won't fall out!

CHAPTER 4

On some coasters, the car is attached to the bottom of the track. Without a floor under your feet, you feel like you're flying!

Keeping It Safe

Roller coaster designers know a lot about physics. They also use their imaginations. They create coasters as big and as thrilling as possible.

Most importantly, designers want their roller coasters to be safe. Roller coaster cars have three sets of wheels. One set fits into the track. Another runs along the sides. The third runs under the track. The car is securely attached. Brakes on the tracks slow down the car or stop it at the station. A lap bar or safety belt keeps you safe in your seat. Workers check the cars and coaster

Experts use special equipment and test dummies to check the safety of rides.

every morning before a park opens. If a park closes for the winter, workers use that time to fix the ride. The roller coaster cars are stored out of the snowy weather.

Attendants use a control panel to make sure the ride runs as it should.

Today, roller coasters run with the help of computers. Computers control the brakes. Computers can also make sure that two cars keep a safe distance apart. They can sense if all the passengers have locked their lap bars. Passengers need to do their part to be safe, too. Read and follow the rules for the ride. If you are not tall enough, don't ride it. Standing on your toes doesn't count!

Amusement park rides are called thrill rides for a reason. They're thrilling!

Pay attention to signs. They show you when you're tall enough to safely ride.

YOU MUST BE THIS TALL TO RIDE THIS RIDE

48″

If you are tall enough, climb on in! Pull down the lap bar and get ready. You are going to whoosh through hills, turns, and loops. Enjoy the ride!

21

Glossary

amusement park [uh-MYOOZ-muhnt PAHRK] a place with games, rides, and other fun activities

centripetal force [sen-TRIP-i-tl FOHRS] the force acting toward the center of a curved path that keeps you moving along the path

designers [di-ZAHY-ners] people who create and plan a building or structure

dioramas [dayh-uh-RAM-uhs] a painted background and three-dimensional figures or objects to show a scene

energy [en-er-JEE] the ability to make something happen

gravity [GRAV-i-tee] a force that pulls objects toward each other

lap bar [LAP BAHR] the safety bar on a roller coaster that acts like a seat belt

launches [LAWNCH-es] shoots out quickly

motor [MOH-ter] a machine that uses energy to make something work or move

parallel [PER-ah-lel] lying in the same direction and the same distance apart

physics [FIZ-iks] the study of how objects move

spiral [SPAHY-ruhl] winding around a center point

Books to Discover

Green, Dan. *Physics*. New York: Kingfisher, 2008.

Hopwood, James. *Cool Gravity Activities: Fun Science Projects About Balance*. Edina, MN: ABDO Publishing Company, 2008.

Koll, Hilary, and Steve Mills. *Using Math to Design a Roller Coaster*. Milwaukee, WI: Gareth Stevens Publishing, 2006.

Newton, Joan. *Gravity in Action: Roller Coasters!* New York: Rosen Classroom, 2009.

Schaefer, Adam Richard. *Roller Coasters*. Mankato, MN: Capstone Press, 2005.

Websites to Explore

American Coaster Enthusiasts: Roller Coaster History
www.aceonline.org/CoasterHistory/

Amusement Park Physics: Roller Coaster
www.learner.org/interactives/parkphysics/coaster.html

Coaster Quest www.coasterquest.com

Roller Coaster Data Base www.rcdb.com/

Index

About the Author

Dana Meachen Rau is the author of more than 250 books for children. She has written about many nonfiction topics from her home office in Burlington, Connecticut. Mrs. Rau only likes to ride roller coasters when she feels safely strapped in. Her son, on the other hand, will climb in any coaster he's tall enough to ride.

With thanks to the Reading Consultants:

Nanci R. Vargus, Ed.D., is an assistant professor of elementary education at the University of Indianapolis.

Beth Walker Gambro is an adjunct professor at the University of Saint Francis in Joliet, Illinois.